# Programming Python: Start Learning Python Today, Even If You've Never Coded Before (A Beginner's Guide)

# Table of Contents

# Chapter 1) Learning Programming with Python

The Python programming language was created by Guido van Rossum in the late 1980s. In contrast to other popular languages such as C, C++, Java, and C#, the main advantage of Python over other programming languages like C++, Java, etc. is that is that it provides a simple yet powerful syntax. It is used to develop software at organizations like Google, CERN, Yahoo, Industrial Light and Magic and many others. Great things can be accomplished with Python if you are an experienced programmer. But the beauty of python lies in the fact that it is also accessible to beginners and gives them the freedom of tackling problems more quickly as compared to other, more complicated languages.
You can find detailed information about Python which includes the links for downloading the latest version for Mac OS X, Microsoft Windows and Linux at
http://www.python.org

**What is python?**
Python is a programming language that has multiple paradigms. It is an object-oriented and structured programming language. It includes a number of language features and supports aspect-oriented programming and functional programming which includes metaprogramming and many other magic methods. It supports many other paradigms that are supported with the help of extensions. This further includes logic programming.

**Most important features of python:**
- **It is easy to use:** There are a few to do things in python. These things are simple. It works on a simple philosophy and that is getting more tasks done easily and quickly employing a minimal mental overhead.
- **Powerful:** Its features are well equipped to meet all the ends required by a powerful programming language. It is the reason why major companies of the

world like Microsoft, IBM and Yahoo have been attracted to it.

- **Object Oriented:** Python is object oriented and this means that python uses programming techniques encapsulating the code within objects.
- **It is a glue language:** Python being a glue language implies that the the complete application need not be written in the language, rather the language for orchestrating modules that are written in other languages is used which enable them to work together for forming the application. Being a glue language, makes it easy to do because of a convenient syntax, data munging, positive backup for inter-process communication and so on.
- **Python Runs everywhere:** Python is available for all major operating systems. You can use python for most of the operating systems. For all implementations, the same source code runs unchanged.
- **Open source language:** Python is freely usable as well as distributable and can be even used for commercial purposes.

  In order to get a copy of python, go to http://www.python.org and download python. Choose the version carefully and avoid choosing the older 2.x version. Choose the 3.x version. After this, execute the installer, and interact well agreeing to all the choices that are default.
- **Idle:** The Python interpreter is the program translating python instructions and then executing them. This interpreter is easy for developing as it is embedded in many larger programs. This interpreter is embedded in a number of larger programs that make it particularly easy to develop the python programs. This kind of programming environment is known as Idle. The Idle is python's standard distribution part.

**The following section explains Idle for each operating system:**

5

**Windows:** In the Python folder, you must see icon for the Idle31Shortcut .Double click on this shortcut and you will see that an Idle window appears.

**Mac OS X:** Python's new version and the Idle must be be in a MacPython 3.x which will be in the Applications folder. For Mac OS X, it is better to start idle from a terminal. But the current directory must be your Python folder.

There are several parts of an Idle that can be chosen to display and they are within its window. As per the configuration, Idle can show one of the two windows: Python Shell Window or the Edit window.

**Edit window:** Most likely, you will first see the the edit window.

**Python Shell Window:** In the Edit window, go to run and after that select PYTHON SHELL, for opening the Python Shell Window. After this, close the Edit Window.

**>>> prompt:** This prompt tells that the Idle is waiting for something to be typed.

# Chapter 2) Values and Variables

In this chapter, the building blocks for python development have been explained in detail. The following points are explained in detail in this chapter.
• Numeric values
• Variables
• Assignment
• Identifiers
• reserved words

**Integer Values**
Integers are whole numbers that do not have any fractional parts, and can be zero, positive or negative. Examples are: −19, 0, and 5. But numbers like 7.8, 9.9000 are not integers, as they are not whole numbers. Integer values can be used by Python programs.
To illustrate the use of integer values, consider the Python statement
**print(5)**

It prints the value 5. Other types of expressions apart from the integer expressions are also supported by python. An expression is a statement and  not a complete Python statement by itself. So it can not be called a program. A Python expression can be directly evaluated by the interpreter.5 can be directly typed into the interpreter shell:

**Python 3.x (default, dec 18 2014, 21:13:15) [MSC v.1500 32 bit (Intel)] 0 32
Type "help", "copyright", "credits", or "license" for more information.
>>>5
5
>>>**

Both statements and expressions can be evaluated by the interactive shell.Here, the expression 5 evaluates to 5. The

read, eval, print loop is executed by the shell. It implies that the sole activity of the interactive shell consists of
1. Reading the text that is entered.
2. Evaluating the input of the user in the context of what has been entered up by the user at that point.
3. Lastly, to print what is has evaluated by the input of the user.

If the user inputs a 5, it is interpreted as 5 by the shell. But if y= 10 is entered by the user, it will be a statement and will not have an overall value of itself. As an output, nothing is printed by the shell. When the user enters y, the evaluation of y, that is 10 is printed by the shell. If x is entered by the user, an error is reported by the shell since x is not defined in a previous interaction.

Consider the following example: It shows the use of quote marks for an integer:
**>>> 19**
**19**
**>>> "19"**
**' 19'**
**>>> ' 19'**
**' 19'**
**>>> "Andy"**
**' Andy'**
**>>> ' Andy'**
**' Andy'**
**>>>Andy**
**Trackback (most recent call last):**
**File "<stdin>", line 1, in <module>**
**NameError: name 'Andy' is not defined**

The expression Andy which was without quotes was rejected by the interpreter due to missing quotation marks. It should be noted that the expressions 5 and '5' are different. The first one represents an integer expression and the other represents a string expression. All Python expressions have a type. The kind of expression is indicated by its type. Sometimes a class is used to denote an xpression. We have considered only strings and integers for now. Any Python xpression's type is revealed by the built in function.

```
>>> type(5)
<class 'int'>
>>> type('5')
<class 'str'>
```

The type name int is associated with integer expressions in Python and str is associated with string expressions. An integer's string representation is converted to an actual integer by the built in int function, and an integer expression is converted to a string by the str function.

```
>>> 3
3
>>> str(3)
' 3'
>>> ' 7'
' 7'
>>> int( ' 7')
7
```

The string value '3' is evaluated by str(3), and the integer value 7 is evaluated by the int('7'). You can represent any integer in the string form, but the reverse is not always true:

```
>>> str(2024)
'2024'
>>> int ('son')
Trackback (most recent call last) :
File "<stdin>", line 1, in <module>
ValueError: invalid literal for int() with base 10: 'son'
>>> int('5.4' )
Trackback (most recent call last) :
File  "<stdin>", line 1, in <module>
ValueError: invalid literal for int() with base 10: '5.4'
```

In the Python programming, both mom and 5.4 do not represent integer expressions that are valid. So you can conclude that if the string contents are a valid integer number they can be safely applied to the int function for producing the represented integer. Consider the example:

```
>>> 6 +20
26
>>> '6' + '20'
'620'
>>> 'abcd' + 'xyz'
'abcdxyz'
```

The 6 + 20 expression has a totally different result from '6' + '20'. The two strings are spliced together by the plus operator through a process termed as concatenation. But you can not mix the two types directly.

**Variables and Assignment**
As you already know that variables are used for the representation of any numbers. It goes in the same way for python except the fact that Python variables may also be used for the representation of values other than numbers.
**Assignment statement:** An assignment statement is a statement that is used for the association of any value with variable. The symbol = is called the assignment operator and is the main key to the assignment operator.
For example:

```
y=10
print(y)
```

The statement y=10 performs the function of assigning the value 10 to the variable y. This statement makes the type of y as int since it has been bounded to an integer value. A variable can be assigned and reassigned as often as necessary.
• **print(y)**
If you type print statement, it prints the current value of the variable y. It should be noted that the lack of quotation marks

is very important here. If the value of y is 10 , then the statement.

**print(y)**

will print 10 as the value of the variable y, but the statement

**print('y')**

prints y.

The assignment operator (=) has a different meaning than the meaning that it has in mathematics.( =), in mathematics means that the expression on the left equals to the expression on the right.But in Python, (=) means that the variable on the left takes the value mentioned on the right side.Consider the statement:

**5 = y**

In this statement, the value of 5 is reassigned. However, this can not be done because 5 can not take any other value and hence it is not possible to change. It attempts to reassign the value of the literal integer value 5, but this cannot be done because 5 is always 5 and cannot be changed. Typing such statement produces error.

**IDENTIFIERS**

An identifier is used for naming things. It is used for naming things like classes, functions as well as methods. We list some of the features of Identifiers:

- They should contain a minimum of one character.
- The first character of an identifier should alphabetic letter (any case) or an underscore
  **ABCabc_**
- The other characters can be alphabetic characters (any case), a digit or an underscore.
  **ABCDabcd_01234.**

- You can not use any other characters (spaces included) in identifiers.
- Reserved words can not be used in an identifier.

The following will explain valid and invalid identifiers:
- y, y2, cool, cool_22, and FLAG are examples of valid identifiers.
- The examples here exemplify invalid identifiers: sub-total (using dash is not legal in an identifier), second entry (using space is not a legal ), 5all (it starts with a digit which is not allowed), #2 (you can use pound sign in an identifier), and class (using class is not allowed as it is a reserved word).

**Reserved words:** A number of words are reserved for special use by python that could be used as identifiers. Such words are called **keywords or reserved words**. These reserved words are special and are employed for defining the Python programs structure. Fortunately, if you accidentally attempt to use one of the reserved words as a variable name within a program, the interpreter issues an error when a reserved word is used as a variable. For example if you type

**>>> class= 10**
**the interpreter shows a syntax error.**
**>>> print ('My best friend print')**
**My best friend print**
**>>> print**
**<built-in function print>**
**>>> type (print)**
**<class 'built_function_or_method'>**
**>>> print = 69**
**>>> print**
**69**
**>>> print ('My best friend print')**
**Traceback (most recent call last):**
** File "<stdin>", line 1, in <module>**
**TypeError: 'int' object is not callable**
**>>> Type (print)**

**<class 'int'>**

Here we used the name print as a variable. In doing so it lost its original behavior as a function to print the console. While we can reassign the names print, str, type, etc., it generally is not a good idea to do so. Not only can a function name can be reassigned, but a variable can be assigned to a function.

**>>> you_bind = print**
**>>> you_bind('hi from you_bind!')**
**hi from you_bind!**

After binding my_print to print, we can use my_print is exactly the same way as the built-in print function. Python is a language that considers the case that has been used and identifiers also consider the case in which a variable or any other word is typed. For example calling is different from Calling in case of python.

**Floating-point Types**
A number of times, we need to use fractions. In Python non-integer values are supported and are termed as floating point numbers. Float is used to denote floating point numbers in python. Consider the example below:

**>>> a = 6.74**
**>>> a**
**6.74**
**>>> type (a)**
**<class 'float'>**

The type has been denoted as float meaning that the number is a floating point number.

# Chapter 3) Functions

A function can be defined as a block of reusable, organized code which is used for performing an action. They offer a better reuse of code and a better application modularity. Python offers a number of built-in functions such as print() and others. It gives you the freedom to build your own functions. They are termed as *user-defined functions/ predefined functions*.

**How to define a function:**

Depending on the required functionality, a function can be defined. Here are simple rules to define a function in Python:

The Function block starts with a keyword 'def'. The name of the function and parentheses ( ( ) ) follow 'def'. All the arguments or input parameters must be inserted inside the parentheses. Within every function, the code block begins with a colon (:) and is indented. Within every function, the code block is indented and begins with a colon(:). return [expression] is used for exiting a function. A return statement without arguments means return None by default.

**The syntax of the function:**

**def the name of function( condition 1,condition 2 ):**

  **the code in the function**

**return [expression]**


The behavior of the parameters is positional. They must be informed in the order as you define them.

The following example explains how a function is used:

**def heya():**

```
    print "heya"

    return 8657
```

**This is how this function is used:**

**print heya()**

**It gives the output as:**

**heya**

**8657**

The steps below will  explain what happened in the above program

In the first step, the function named 'heya' is created by running 'def heya()'

The execution of the function 'heya' takes place on running the line 'print heya()'

On screen 'heya' is printed by the function 'heya' and after that 8657 is returned back to the actual program.

'print 8657' is now seen by the actual program and the number '8657' is printed.

**Some important functions:**

**Built-In Functions:**
The built-in functions are placed in a module known as _builtin_. The most common among them are explained one by one:

**type:** This function is used for returning any object's data type. The types module contains the possible data types. The following function

```
>>> type(6)
   <type 'int'>
```

**str:** This function is used for the conversion of any data type into a string.

```
>>> str(5)
   '5'
```

## Some Mathematical Functions:

The standard math module provides much of the functionality of a scientific calculator. Table below lists only a few of the available functions. The mathematical functions are included in the math module. Below is the list of some of them:

| | |
|---|---|
| **exp** | This function performs computing e raised a power. |
| **sqrt** | This function finds the square root of a number. |
| **log10** | This function calculates a number's common logarithm. |
| **log** | This function calculates a number's natural logarithm. |
| **pow** | This function adds to the power of a number. |
| **cos** | This function calculates the cosine value in radians |
| **radians** | This function is used for the conversion from degrees to radians. |
| **degrees** | This function is used for the conversion of radians to degrees. |
| **fabs** | This function if used for the calculation of a number's absolute value. |

## Time Functions

The time package contains a number of functions that relate to time. We will consider two: clock and sleep.

The clock function allows us measure the time of parts of a program's execution. The clock returns a floating-point value representing elapsed time in seconds. On Unix-like systems (Linux and Mac OS X), clock returns the numbers of seconds elapsed since the program began executing. Under Microsoft Windows, clock returns the number of seconds since the first call to clock. In either case, with two calls to the clock function we can measure elapsed time. The program below measures how long it takes a user to enter a character from the keyboard.

There are a number of functions that are related to time. For example: sleep and clock.

```
from time import clock

print("Please type in fullName: ", end="")
initiate_time = clock()
fullName = input()
taken = clock() - initiate_time
print(fullName, "The overall time taken by you is", taken, "seconds")
```

## Random Numbers

The Python random module contains a number of standard functions that programmers can use for working with pseudorandom numbers. Sometimes an application needs a random behavior. Random numbers are mostly used in simulations and games. There are a number of functions that are included in the random module. You may employ them while when you make a program using pseudo random numbers. Some of these are:

**randrange** It is used for returning a pseudorandom integer in a particular range.

| random | It is used for returning floating-point number that lies in within 0 $\le$ x < 1 and is pseudorandom |
|---|---|
| seed | It is used for setting seed which is a random number. |

# Chapter 4) Classes

You may define a class as a container and you are able to use anything that is inside this class. In a function, whatever values you create are lost after the function is exit.
The following gives the generalized way of how a class can be created:

**class name of class:**
    **[first statement]**
    **[second statement]**
    **[third statement]**
    **[etc]**

No one likes to do something that has already been completed once. Functions solve this problem in python. Once you have written a code and want to reuse it, you can use a function for it.
But there are certain shortcomings and limitations that a function has. The first thing is that they can store values like a variable does. But not to worry because Python supports object oriented programming and can make the variables and functions work in conjunction with each other. This enables them to be altered as per requirement. This is done with the help of a class.


```
class formation:
  def __init__(self,a,b):
     self.a = a
     self.b = b
  explanation = "Formation is not described so far"
  writer = "The formation is not claimed so far "
  def perimeter(self):
  return 2 * self.a + 2 * self.b
  def area(self):
  return self.a * self.b

  def describe(self,msg):
```

```
    self.explanation = msg
def writerName(self,msg):
    self.writer = text
def scalesize(self,scale):
    self.a = self.a * scale
self.b = self.b * scale
```

In this program, a class named formation  has been created along with the operation that we can do with that formation. The formation has width(a),  height(b), a perimeter as well as an area.

For the creation of an instance of formation when the function __init__ is run. In order to refer what is inside class, self is used.elf.  For any function, the first parameter is self. In order to access a function and variable in the class, the name of these functions and variables should be preceded by self and then a full stop.

**How to use a class**
Now that you know how to create a class, you must also know how to use it. The following example explains how.

**rect = formation(50,10)**

**Now we explain what is actually been done:**
In the above equation, firstly an instance is made by giving it a name. In this case, we have given the name-formation and the values that in the brackets are passed to _init_ function which runs and spits an instance's class. Here the instance is given the name rect.

Rect now becomes a collection of functions and variables and is self-contained. We use rect for accessing the variables and functions that belong to the class from outside. We can do the following from the code that has been done above:

```
#in order to find the area:
print rect.area()

#in order to find the perimeter:
print rect.perimeter()

#in order to describe rect
rect.describe("rect is a rectangle")

#making rect 80% small
rect.scaleSize(0.8)
```

Thus we can call a number of instances from the class formation.

**Lingo:**

There are some lingos that are related to Python. They are explained as:

- When a class is firstly described, it is defined.
- Encapsulation is the ability of grouping similar variables and functions.
- An attribute is a variable that is a class.
- A class is a data structure holding data and methods for processing that data.

**Inheritance**

Using the inheritance is not a difficult job in python. We make a new class which is based on the main class or the parent class. Everything is drawn from the parent and other things can also be included in the new class. Lets do this with the formation class.

```python
class formation:
    def __init__(self,a,b):
        self.a = a
        self.b = b
    explanation = "The formation is not described so far"
    writer = "The formation is not claimed so far"
    def area(self):
        return self.a * self.b
    def perimeter(self):
        return 2 * self.a + 2 * self.b
    def describe(self,msg):
        self.description = msg
    def authorName(self,msg):
        self.writer = msg
    def scaleSize(self,scale):
        self.a = self.b * scale
    self.b = self.b * scale
```

Suppose, we want to make a new class( say, squ), using the class formation, we can do it like this:

```python
class Squ(formation):
    def __init__(self,a):
        self.a = a
        self.b = a
```

Defining this class is just like the way a class is normally defined with the only difference being that in the brackets, the parent class is put. By using inheritance, a parent class can be

22

used in a more efficient manner and a new class can be created more easily inheriting the properties of the parent class.

## Pointers and Dictionaries of Classes

In there are two instances that have the same value on the right hand side, then both instances become equal that is instanceX = instanceY. Here instanceX is pointing to instanceY. And either of the name can be used to access class instance. The last thing covered is the dictionaries of classes. An instance can be assigned to a dictionary entry using a pointer. This enables the existence of any number of instances that can exist when a program is done. The program below will explain this furthermore:

```
dictionary = {}

# Then, create some instances of classes in the dictionary:
dictionary["TripleSquare 1"] = TripleSquare(3)
dictionary["large rect"] = Shape(1000,350)

#You can now use them like a normal class:
print dictionary["large rect"].perimeter()

dictionary["TripleSquare 1"].writerName("Peter Parker")
print dictionary["TripleSquare 1"].writer
```

# Chapter 5) Expressions and Conditional Execution

Expressions can be exemplified by a literal value like 56 and a variable like y. Values and variables can be combined with operators to form More complex expressions can be formed by combining values and variables. In chapter 2, we saw how we can use the + operator to add integers and concatenate strings. Various expressions along with their strings are given below:

| Expression | Meaning |
|---|---|
| a + b | a added to b, provided a and b are numbers |
| | a concatenated to b, if a and b are strings |
| a - b | a take away b, provided a and b are numbers |
| a * b | a times b, if a and b are numbers |
| | a concatenated with itself b times, when a is a string and b is an integer |
| a / b | a divided by b, if a and b are numbers |
| a // b | Floor of a divided by b, if a and b are numbers |
| a % b | Remainder of a divided by b, when x and y are numbers |
| a ** b | a raised to b power, if a and b are numbers |

Consider the command:
- **print(valuea, '+', valueb, '=', sum)**

The values of the three variables are printed by this statement along with some additional decoration for having a clearer output. In this chapter, the constructs enabling a program to be optionally executed are explained in detail.

## Boolean Expressions

Boolean expressions are used for evaluating numeric values. It can take only two values:true or false. They are the simplest expressions in Python . We can see in a Python interactive shell:

```
>>> False
False
>>> True
True
>>> type(False)
<class 'bool'>
>>> type(True)
<class 'bool'>
```

## Python relational expressions

| Expression | Meaning |
| --- | --- |
| a == b | True if a is equal to b ;false otherwise. |
| a < b | True if a is less than b; false otherwise. |
| a <= b | True if a is less than or equal to b; false, otherwise. |
| a > b | True if a is less than b; false otherwise. |
| a != b | True if a is not equal to b; false otherwise. |

## Example Relational expressions:

| Expression | Value |
| --- | --- |
| 20 < 25 | True |
| 20 >= 25 | False |
| a < 200 | True if a is less than 200; False otherwise |
| a != b | True when a and b are equal. |

## Logical Expressions

## And operator:

This operator becomes true only when both the operands become true then the condition becomes true.

## OR operator:

The operator becomes true only when either of the two operands are non zero.

## NOT operator:

The NOT operator is used to reverse the expression's truth value.

## Conditional Statements:

### The Simple if Statement
The if statement allows optional execution of the code. The syntax for a simple if statement is

**if expression:**

**the conditional statement(s)**

**else:**

**the conditional statement(s)**

**example:**

**y = 2**

**if y == 2:**

**print "It is the result"**

**The result will be 'It is the result'.**

26

## The if/else Statement:

There is an optional clause that an 'if' statement can have. It is the else clause and is executed when the Boolean condition is not satisfied.

The general form of an if/else statement is

**if:**
    **the statement**
**else:**
    **the statement**

**Example:**
**b = 6**
**if b > 6:**
    **print "This is correct ."**
**else:**
    **print "This is not correct."**
**elif statement:**
  **'elseif' can be used instead of 'else if'. The following statement explains it.**
**z = 2**
**if z > 7:**
    **print "Something is wrong"**
**elif z < 7:**
    **print "Nothing is wrong"**

The syntax of if, elseif, else can be represented as:
**if {conditions}:**
    **{this code is run}**
**elif {conditions}:**
    **{this code is run}**
**elif {conditions}:**
    **{this code is run}**
**else:**
    **{this code is run}**

## Nested Conditionals

We can make a nested conditional by combining a series of else/if and elif statements. The following example will explain creating nested conditionals using if, else/if, elif:

Using only if:
```
value = eval(input("Enter a number in between 0...5: ")
if value >= 0:              # First check
if value <=:                # Second check
      print("Is good")
print("Finish")
```

Sometimes , it is not possible to simplify a logic using only the if statement, in such cases the else/if or elif conditions are used. This is explained as follows:

```
value = eval(input("Enter a number in between 0...20: ")
if value >= 0:                                        #
First check
if value <= 20:
      # Second check
print(value, "number entered is valid")
else:
      print(value, "number entered is not valid")
else:
print(value, "please enter a greater number")
print("Finish")
```

**Multi-way Decision Statements**
In multi-way dimension statements, we can choose between two execution paths. The following example will explain how they are being used:

```
value = eval(input("Enter a number in between 10...15: "))
if value < 10:
```

```
        print("Too small")
else:
        if value == 10:
            print("ten")
        else:
            if value == 11:
                print("eleven")
            else:
                if value == 12:
                    print("twelve")
                else:
                    if value == 13:
                        print("thirteen")
                    else:
                        if value == 14:
                            print("fourteen")
                        else:
                            if value == 15:

        print("fifteen")
                            else:
                                print("Number is
larger than 15")
print("Done")
```

One of the eight messages is printed by this statement depending on the input given by the user.

# Chapter 6) Iteration

Iteration means the repetition of a code sequence. It helps to solve many programming problems. A combination of Iteration as well as conditional execution lays the foundation for algorithm construction. Various statements like the while statement, the 'for' statement are used for iterations. This chapter mainly explains the statements that enable iteration.

**The while Statement**
This statement works as a control a while loop is a control flow loop enabling the repeated execution of a code till the initialized counter.It can be explained as:

```
count = 0               # Start the counter
while count <= 10:      # Limit of
the counter
    print(count)        # Display the
counter and then
    count += 1          # Increase the
counter by one
```

In the lines 0,1, 2, 3, 4 the counter is firstly initialized to 10 and the variable count is display.

**print(count)**
**count += 1**

are executed ten times. After each redisplay of the variable count, the program increments it by one. Eventually (after five iterations), the condition count <= 10 will not be correct, and the block is no longer executed.

**while count <= 10** means that the expression after is the condition determining whether the statement block continues to execute. The code block  is executed again and again till the condition is true.When the condition is incorrect, the loop ends.

## Definite Loops vs. Indefinite Loops

```
x = 0
while x <= 5:
print(x)
n += 1
```

The above example specifies a definite loop, as the number of times the loop is repeated can be predicted.

```
done = False              # Enter the loop at least
once
while not done:
entry = eval(input())    # Get value from user
if entry == 99:          # Did you enter the correct
number?
done = True               # You will get out if you
had
else:
print(entry)             # print the number and
continue
```

In the above example, the number of iterations performed by the loop during its execution can not be predicted.The value matching (99) is known both before and during the loop, but the variable entry can be anything the user enters. The user could choose to enter 0 exclusively or enter 999 immediately and be done with it. The while statement, above is an example of an indefinite loop.

### The for Statement
The 'for' statement is used for iteration over a range of values. The values can be either a numeric range, or elements of a string, tuple or list. The statement given below explains the use of a 'for' loop:

```
for m in range(1, 20):
```

```
print(x)
```

The expression range (1, 20) creates an iterable that enables the for loop to assign to the variable n the values 1, 2, 20. During the first iteration of the loop, n's value is 1 within the block. In the loop's second iteration, n has the value of 2 and so the loop goes on till it reaches 20.

**Nested Loops**
Just like with if statements, while and for blocks can contain arbitrary Python statements, including other loops. A loop can therefore be nested within another loop. The following example prints a multiplication table on the screen using nested for loops.

```
#
Multiplication
table to 5 x 5
                  # Print the
                  column heading
print(" 1  2  3  4  5 ")
print("  +.............")
for row in range(1, 6):          # 1 <= row
<= 6, table will have 5 rows
if row < 5:
print(" ", end="")
print(row, "| ", end="")
for column in range(1, 6):          #
Table will have 5 columns.
product = row*column;          #
Calculate the product
if product < 25:
print(end=" ")
if product < 5:
print(end=" ")
```

```
print(product, end=" ")                                    #
Display the product
print()
```

## Infinite Loops

An infinite loop is a loop that executes its block of statements repeatedly until the user forces the program to quit. Once the program flow enters the loop's body it cannot escape. Infinite loops are sometimes designed.

Consider the program below that attempts to print all the integers with their associated factors from 1 to 10.

```
                                                    # Getting
                                                    factors of all
                                                    integers
                                                    1...MAX
        MAX = 10                                    # MAX is
given a value of 10
        x = 1                                       # Starting
with 1
        while x <= MAX:                             # Cannot
exceed MAX
        factor = 1
        print(end=str(n) + ': ')                    # Integer
that is being examined
        while factor <= x:
        if x % factor == 0:                              # To
check if factor of x
        print(factor, end=' ')                      # If it has
factors, display them
        factor += 1                                 # Getting
factors of next number
        print()                                     # Move to
next line for next x
        X += 1
```

33

It displays

        **1: 1**
        **2: 1 2**
        **3: 1**

In general, the execution of the while statement takes place till the condition no longer remains true. This checking takes place at the loop's top; hence there is no immediate exiting of the loop in case of a false condition because of some action in the middle of the program. Normally this type of behaviour is not a problem since the intention is of executing all the statements in a body just like an individual unit. But there are times when immediately exiting the body or rechecking the condition from the loop's middle instead. Continues and break statements are provided by Python to offer give programmers giving more flexibility for controlling the loops logic.

**The break statement**

The break statement is provided by python for implementing the control logic of middle exiting. This statement leads to the immediate exiting from the loop's body.

**# Allow the user to enter a sequence of non-negative**

**# numbers. The user ends the list with a negative**

**# number. At the end the sum of the non-negative**

**# numbers entered is displayed. The program prints**

**# zero if the user provides no non-negative numbers.**

**entry = 0      # Make sure that the loop is started**

```python
sum = 0        # Starting the sum

               # Ask the user to enter an input
               print("Please write the numbers for
               addition,ends list of the negative
               numbers:")

while True:                    # Loop will continue
infinite

entry = eval(input())

if entry < 0:                  # Check for the negative
number

break                          # if negative,end the
loop

addition += entry              # insert new value to
sum

print("Result =", addition)    # Output the result
```

As the while condition can not be false, the only way of getting out of the loop is the break statement. When the programmer enters a negative number, the execution of the break statement takes place. The immediate exiting of the loop takes place on encountering the break statement. The statements that follow the break exit immediately.

The following program uses break statements in place of the Boolean done variable.

```python
print("I am having problem with my laptop, it is not working")

while True:
```

```python
print("Is laptop making any noice or blinking(hard disk, etc.)")

choice = input(" hard disk light? (y/n):")

if choice == 'n':    # Laptop does not have any battery power

choice = input("Is power cable plugged in? (y/n):")

if choice == 'n':    # Power cable is not connected, connect it with the laptop

print("Connect the charging wire")

else:                # Power cable is already plugged i

choice = input("Toggle the power switch in \"on\" position? (y/n):")

if choice == 'n':            # Knob is switched off, toggle it on

print("Please switch on the power.")

else:                        # Power is on

choice = input("Is the laptop having fuse issues? (y/n):")

if choice == 'n':            # Does not have fuse

choice = input("Is the outlet OK? (y/n):")

if choice == 'n':            # Repair the regulator

print("Look for the status of the regulator ")

print("if regulator not working")
```

```python
        print("switch to different regulator ")
    else:
        print("Contact your laptop technician")
        break
    else:                           # Look for the fuse
        print("Use different fuse")
        print("required")
    else:                           # Laptop have power
        print("Contact your laptop technician")
        break
```

The less use of the break statement must be made since an exception is introduced into the loop's normal control logic. In an ideal condition, each loop must have only one entry and exit point.

While some has a single exit point (the break statement), programmers commonly use break statements within while statements with conditions that are not always true. In such a while loop, adding a break statement adds an extra exit point (the top of the loop where the condition is checked is one point, and the break statement is another).

Using multiple break statements within a single loop is particularly dubious and should be avoided. Why have the break statements at all if its use is questionable and it is dispensable? The above program is fairly simple, so the restructuring of this program is straightforward; in general, the effort may complicate the logic a bit and require the introduction of an additional Boolean variable. Any program that uses a break statement can be rewritten so that the break statement is not used. Any loop of the form

**while condition A :**

**statement A**

**statement B**

**...**

**statement X**

**if condition B:**

**statement N+A**

**statement N+B**

**...**

**statement N+Y**

**break**

**statement N+Y+A**

**statement N+Y+B**

**...**

**statement N+Y+P**


can be rewritten as


**done = false**

```
while not done and condition A :
statement A
statement B
...
statement N;
if condition B :
statement N+A
statement N+B
...
statement N+M
done = true
else:
statement N+M+A
statement N+M+B
...
statement N+M+P
```

A Boolean variable is introduced by the no-break version and there is more complication in the control logic of the loop. More space is used by the no-break version and the logic is more complicated. It is very difficult writing the code correctly if the control logic is more complex. During some situations, even after the "one entry point, one exit point" principle is violated; the simple break statement might be a good option for the control of loop.

## The continue Statement

The continue statement is similar to the break statement. In a program, when there is an encounter of the break statement in a loop's body, the rest of the statements are skipped and the loop is exit. When the loop encounters a continue statement, the rest of the statements that are inside the body are left. Even though the statements are skipped, checking of the loop condition takes place to decide whether the loop should be continued or not. If the condition of the loop is not false, exiting of the loop does not take place. Rather the execution of the loop takes place at the top.

The code below shows how the continue statement can be used.

**addition = 0**

**complete = False;**

**while not complete:**

**val = eval(input("Enter any number greater than zero and smaller than thousand:"))**

**if val < 0:**

**print("Number smaller than zero", val, "neglect")**

**continue;**

**if val != 999:**

**print("Counting", val)**

**addition += val**

**else:**

```
complete = (val == 999);
```

```
print("addition =", addition)
```

Now consider the following code, it works exactly like the above code but the "continue" has been eliminated.The break is statement is used less frequently than the continue statement as it is easier transforming the code into a form that does not employ continue.

```
addition = 0
```

```
complete = False;
```

```
while not done:
```

```
val = eval(input("Enter any number greater than zero and smaller than thousand:"))
```

```
if val < 0:
```

```
print("Number smaller than zero", val, "neglect")
```

```
else:
```

```
if val != 999:
```

```
print("Counting", val)
```

```
addition += val
```

```
else:
```

```
complete = (val == 999);
```

```
print("addition =", addition)
```

In fact any loop body of the form

```
while condition A:
statement A
statement B
...
statement N
if condition B:
statementn+A
statementn+B
...
statement N+M
continue
statement N+M+A
statement N+M+B
...
statement N+M+P
```

can be rewritten as

```
while condition A:
statement A
statement B
```

```
...

statement N

if condition B:

statementn+A

statementn+B

...

statement N+M

else:

statement N+M+A

statement N+M+B

...

statement N+M+P
```

The else version is as complicated as the continue version. Therefore, there is not a very good reason for using the continue statement. In some cases, we add the continue statement at the last moment to a loop body for handling an exceptional condition that was unnoticed in the beginning. If the loop has a long body, you can easily add a conditional statement near the loop's top. Hence, the continue statement is not a great option for the programmer. It is therefore better to prefer the else version.

## Infinite Loops

An infinite loop performs the repeated execution of its statements block until is forced by the user to quit. Once the flow of program enters the body of the loop, it is not possible to escape. However, for new programmers, it is quite a possibility that they create the infinite loops accidentally and logic errors are represented in the programs that they make.

Intentional infinite loops must be made obvious. The example below explains this in detail:

**while True:**

**# It will be executed infinite times. . .**

The Boolean true is always true; hence it is not possible that the condition of the loop is false. The only way of exiting the loop is through a break statement, return statement.

Writing the intentional infinite loops correctly is easy. Infinite accidental loops are very common, but for the new programmers, it might be confusing for repair and diagnosing.Consider the example below, it will explain this point a further more:

Consider the following program, this program attempts to print all the integers with their associated factors from 1 to 10.

**MAXIMUM = 10**          **# MAXIMUM is 10**

**x = 1**          **# Loop will start with 1**

**while x <= MAXIMUM:**          **# Loop cannot go beyond 10**

**factor = 1**          **# 1 is a factor of every integer**

```python
    print(end=str(x) + ': ')        # Current integer under
calculation

    while factor <= x:

        if x % factor == 0:

            print(factor, end=' ')

        factor += 1                 # Check the factors of
next integer

    print()

    x += 1
```

It displays

> 1: 1
>
> 2: 1 2
>
> 3: 1

And after that "hangs" and ignores any input of the user. Such a behavior is a common symptom for an unintentional loop that is infinite. The factors that 1 has are displayed in a proper manner and also the factors of 2. The first factor of 3 displayed correctly and after this the program somehow hangs.

Since the program is short, the problem may be easy to locate. In some programs, though, the error may be challenging to find. Even in the above program, the debugging task is nontrivial since nested loops are involved.

For avoiding infinite loops, we should make sure that some properties are exhibited by the loop:

The condition of the loop should not be a tautology. Consider the example below:

**while x >= 1 or x <= 100:**

**# Rest of the code....**

In the above program the outer loop condition is

**x <= MAXIMUM**

The condition turns out to be false when x equals to 21 and MAXIMUM. As values for x and MAXIMUM can be found that means that the expression is false, this can't be a tautology.

How to check the inner loop condition:

**factor <= x**

We observe that if the factor equals to 3 and x equals to 2, this makes the expression false. Hence such an expression is not a tautology too.

The code that is within the body should modify the program's state in a way or the other for influencing the condition's outcome that is being checked during every iteration. This implies that one of the variables that are employed in the condition has been modified to the code's body. The variables eventually suppose that a condition is made false by a value and the termination of the loop takes place.

In the above same progam the outer loop's condition involves the variables x and MAXIMUM. We observe that we assign 20 to MAXIMUM before the loop and never change it afterward, so to avoid an infinite loop it is essential that x be modified in the loop. Good thing here is that the x increments. x is initially 1 and MAXIMUM is 20, so unless the circumstances arise to make the inner loop infinite, the outer loop eventually should terminate.

The condition of the inner loop uses the variables x as well as a factor. None of the statements that are inside the inner loop modify x, so the modification of the factor in the loop is imperative. Better news is that it is possible to increment the factor in the inner body's loop. The sad part being that the increment operation has been protected within the if statement's body. The one statement present in the inner loop is the if statement. There are further two statements under the if statement as described below:

**while factor <= x:**

**if x % factor == 0:**

**print(factor, end=' ')**

**factor += 1**

No change in the variable factor takes place if the if condition goes false at any instant. Here, if <=x is true, this further remains true. This leads to the creation of loop that is infinite. The statement modifying that the factor should be moved outside the body of the if statement.

**while factor <= x:**

**if x % factor == 0:**

**print(factor, end=' ')**

**factor += 1**

This runs in the correct way:

**1: 1**

**2: 1 2**

**3: 1 3**

**4: 1 2 4**

**5: 1 5**

**6: 1 2 3 6**

**7: 1 7**

**8: 1 2 4 8**

**9: 1 3 9**

**10: 1 2 5 10**

A debugger can be employed for stepping through a program for seeing why and where occurs. There is another way and that is putting the print statements at places for examining the variables values that are involved in controlling the loop. It is possible to augment the original inner loop.

```
while factor <= x:

print('factor =', factor, ' x =', x)

if x % factor == 0:

print(factor, end=' ')
```

```
factor += 1                    # <-- It is having an error
from the original code
```

This is the output that is produced:

**1: factor = 1 n = 1**

**1**

**2: factor = 1 n = 2**

**1 factor = 2 n = 2**

**2**

**3: factor = 1 n = 3**

**1 factor = 2 n = 3**

**factor = 2 n = 3**

**factor = 2 n = 3**

**factor = 2 n = 3**

**factor = 2 n = 3**

**factor = 2 n = 3**

.

.

.

The same line is continued to be played in the program till the execution is interrupted by the user. The output shows that the once factor= 2 n=3, inside the inner loop, the execution of the program gets trapped

1. 2 < 3 is true, so the loop continues and

2. 3 % 2 is equal to 1, so the if statement will not increment factor.

Incrementing the factor every time through the inner loop is imperative; hence the the factor which increments the statement should be moved outside of the guarded body of if. To move it outside will imply that is removed from if statement's block which further implies that is being indented.

The below written program is a different version of our factor finder program that uses nested for loops instead of nested while loops. It is a bit shorter and also ignores the potential for the factor variable that is misplaced. It is so as the loop variable update is automatically handled by the 'for statement'. This is because the 'for' statement automatically handles the loop variable update.

**# List the factors of the integers 1...MAX**

**MAXIMUM = 10                                # MAXIMUM is 10**

**for n in range(1, MAXIMUM + 1):**

**print(end=str(x) + ': ')                    # Current integer**

**for factor in range(1, x + 1):**

**if x % factor == 0:**

**print(factor, end=' ')**

**print()**

# Chapter 8) Dictionaries, Lists, Tuples

## Introduction

Variables store information that can change with time. But when we require a long information list that is to be stored, such as the days of a week or all the sun signs, what are we going to do in python? The solution to this answer is: we will use dictionaries, lists and tuples. This chapter gives a detailed information about dictionaries, lists and tuples. Lists: They are as the name suggests, a list that contains values. The values are numbered from zero that means the first value is given zero number, the second value is given 1 number and so on.

## Dictionaries:

- Lists are what they seem - a list of values. The first one is given the number zero, the second one as 1, the third one as 2, etc. You can delete or add the values in the list. For example: the names of your many dogs.
- Tuples are almost similar to lists, but their values can't be altered. The values that are given initially are fixed for the remaining portion of the program such as the days of a week. Every value begins with zero in the same way as a list.
- Dictionaries, as suggested by the name have the same function as a dictionary. A key represents the word and the value represents the definition such as, a telephone booth.

## Tuples

Making tuples is very easy. A name is given to a tuple and after that the values. The following example will explain tuple.

**sunsigns=
('Capricorn','Aquarius','Pisces','Aries','Taurus','Gemini','Cancer','Leo','Scorpio','Virgo',
'Libra','Sagittarius')**

There is no need to put parentheses. They have only been put to remove confusion. You can also put space after the commas. It doesn't actually affect the statement. In Python, the tuple that we have made will be organized as:

**Tupal indices:**

| Tuple | Index |
|---|---|
| Capricorn | 0 |
| Aquarius | 1 |
| Pisces | 2 |
| Aries | 3 |
| Taurus | 4 |
| Gemini | 5 |
| Cancer | 6 |

| | |
|---|---|
| **Leo** | 7 |
| **Scorpio** | 8 |
| **Virgo** | 9 |
| **Libra** | 10 |
| **Sagittarius** | 11 |

## Lists:

They are almost the same as tuples. The only difference is that the values inside them can be changed. That is the main reason why lists are prefered over tuples. Example, consider you have six dogs, Tom, Dick, Harry, Nik, Ana and Teju. A list using these names can be created as

**Dogs = ['Tom','Dick','Harry,'Nik','Ana','Teju']**

As can be seen this is almost similiar to tuple but square brackets are used instead of parenthesis. If you want to print the fourth dog, you will type:

**print dogs[3]**

If you want to add a value to the list, you will type:

**dogs.append('Gomzi')**

Suppose you want to delete the last dog, you type:

**del dogs[5]**

Dictionaries:

Suppose you want a list of person along with their heights. This can neither be done by list or tuple. Dictionaries come into picture in such cases. The following example will be more helpful in clearing the idea:

**height = {'Nikhil':5.7, \ Ana':5.3, 'Hny':5.0 \ 'Neha':5.5}**

Suppose we want to add entry to dictionary height, it can be dome as

**height['Tejbhan Man'] = 4.11**

Now when we want to remove an entry from the dictionay height, the code for this is

**del height['Tejbhan Man']**

The following is an program that you can practice and learn more about the function:
**ages = {}**


**villain['Thor'] = 79**
**villain['Bruce'] = 25**
**villain['Petter'] = 19**
**villain['Clark'] = 35**


**if villain.has_key('Thor'):**
**  print "Thor is in hero list. He has", \**
**villain['Thor'], "enemy"**

```
else:
    print "Thor is not in the list"

print "Below is a list of the heros in the dictionary:"
print villain.keys()

keys = villain.keys()

print "Heros have following enemies:", \
villain.values()

values = villain.values()

print keys
keys.sort()
print keys

print values
values.sort()
print values


print "The dictionary has", \
len(villain), "number of villain in it."
```

## How to open a file

For opening a text file, certain parameters are passed to open () telling the way in which you want the file to be opened like 'r' stands for read, 'w' for writing, 'r+' includes both writing and reading, 'a' for adding anything to the file. The example below tells us how to open a file named 'windows' and also the file is printed with what is read inside the file.

**openfile = open('pathofwindows', 'r')**
**openfile.read()**

After opening the file the screen will show lots of '/n' signs. This sign represents a command to enter to next line on the output screen. The content in the file is completely unformatted but when it is passed, the output will be completely formatted.

## Other I/O Functions

There are a number of functions that aid you to deal with files. These have a number of uses that give you more freedom and make it easier to do things. Let us consider, readline(), readlines(), close(), write().

**tell ():** There are no parameters for tell() and it performs the function of returning to the cursor location. This is particularly useful when you intend to know what has been referred to by you, where it is located and the cursor control. In order to use it, type namefileobject.tell(). Here namefileobject represents the fileobject's name created while opening the file inopenfile=open (pathofwindows,'r').

**readline ():** It performs the function of reading from where the cursor will be till the line's end. It is particularly helpful in events like progressively going through a particular thing or while going through a log of events. No parameters need to be passed to it but you have an option of telling the maximum number of letters or bytes that are to be read. It is done by inserting a number within brackets. It can be used with objectfilename.readline().

Don't get confused between readlines() and readline(). The only difference between them is that in the former all the lines are read after the cursor, a list is returned in which each element of the list holds the code. It can be used with any file for example consider we have a file, 'touring' we can use the readlines() function as touringobjectname.readlines(). All the lines of the files will displayed as follows

**FirstLine**

**Third Line**

**FourthLine**

**Sixth Line**

the list returned from readlines ()

| Index | Value |
|-------|-------|
| 0 | **first line** |
| 1 | **second line** |
| 2 | **third line** |

| 3 | fourth line |
|---|---|
| 4 | fifth line |
| 5 | sixth line |

**The write ():** This function is used for writing into the file. It begins writing where the cursor is present and starts overwriting the text that is infrontof it. In order to employ the best use of this function, a string can put within the brackets for writing for example:   Consider we have a file named 'hiking', hikingojectname.write('this is a trip').

**Mmm and Pickles:** Pickles in Python are not to be eaten! Instead, they are objects that are saved to a file. Here the object could be a list, tuple, variables, dictionary, etc. You can also pickle a lot of other things but that is of course within limits. You can restore as well as unpickle the objects. Pickling is done with the help of dump() function that is in the pickle module. The example below will better expalin how pickling is done in python.

```
### pickleproject.py
### How an object is pickled

# importing the pickle module
import pickle

# Creation of a pickled object
```

```
# Let us make a list
picklelist = ['1',two,'3','4',five,'easy enough to count?']

# After this a file is created
# replacing name of the file with the intended file
file = open('filename', 'w')

# pickling picklelist
pickle.dump(picklelist,file)

#Complete the pickling by closing the file
file.close()
```

We write the code for pickling an object as pickle.load(object_to pickle, file_object), where 'object_to_pickle' have the object that we want to pickle and 'file_object' contains the object that we want to write. Close the file afterwards and re-open the file with any text file reader.

Now consider we want to unpickle an object:

```
### unpickleproject.py
### unpickle file

# importing the module of pickle
import pickle

# opening a file in order to read
# replace hiking file with the path to the file you
```

```
created in pickletest.py
unpicklefile = open('hiking', 'r')


# loading the pickled list into a new object
unpickledlist = pickle.load(unpicklefile)

# closing the file for the safety purpose
unpicklefile.close()

# Try to  use the list
for item in unpickledlist:
    print item
```

**Modules:**

A module can be defined as a python file having only
definitions of functions, variables and classes. The following
example will help you to have a better understanding of a
module.

```
# Lets take some variable defined:
numbernine = 9
ageofking = 45

# define some functions
def printregards():
    print "regards"

def timesfive(input):
    print input * 5

# define a class
```

```python
class voilin:
  def __init__(self):
    self.type = raw_input("What type of violin is being used?")
    self.weight = raw_input("What weight (in grams)? ")
    self.wood = raw_input("What kind of wood is used (in years)? ")

  def printdescription(self):
    print "This voilin has a/an " + self.wood + " years",
    print self.type, "voilin, " + self.weight, "grams heavy\"."
```

As can be seen from the above program, a module looks quite similar to any Python program.So what is to be done by a Python module? Bits of the the module are imported to other programs. For importing all the functions, variables and classes to other program from moduletest.py, you will need this to be done:

### higherlevelprogram.py
import moduleprogram

Normally, all the import statements are put at the  python file beginning, but it may be anywhere. For using the items that are in the module in the program, you need to use:

print moduletest.woodusedinvoilin
cfcvoilin = moduletest.Voilin()
cfcvoilin.printdetails()

As can be seen, the imported modules behave in a way quite similar to classes.

**Importing items directly to a program:**
In order to avoid the fuss of putting the 'modulename.' every time before the item, only the required module objects can be imported. The 'from' operator is used to do this. It is used as from modulename. The following example further clarifies it:

### ### DIRECTLY IMPORTING ITEMS TO OUR PYTHON PROGRAMS

**from violin import qualityofwood**
**from violin import printregards**

**# We can now use them**
**print qualityofwood**
**printregards()**

What is the benefit of this? You can employ it for making your code more readable. It can also aid in removing the complexity if we are getting into module heap that are further inside modules. By employing this way, you may import anything from a module with the help of modulename import*. It may cause a little problem if you have the same name for items and objects in the module. It may be so with larger modules and can be quite troublesome. This can be done in a better way by importing a module normally and after that assigning the items to a local name:

**clockfive = moduletest.clockfive**

```
# Using the local name
print clockfive(786)
```

This way the crypticness can be removed of and all the items can be had from a certain module.

## Chapter 10) EXCEPTIONS HANDLING in Python

This chapter will cover exception handling and the various aspects related to it.

### What is Exception?

An exception is something occurring while the program execution takes place and disrupts the flow of the instructions of the program. When a situation that can not be handled by the python script occurs, an exception is raised. In short an exception can be defined as a python object representing an error.

### How to handle an exception:

If you have a code that is suspicious, it may lead to an exception. The program can be defended if it is placed in a try: block. An except: statement must be included after the try:block. This is followed by a code block handling the problem to the best of its capacity.

### Syntax:

**Your operations are performed here;**

.....................

**except Exception :**

The execution of the block takes place in case of an exception

**except Exception:**

The execution of the block takes place in case of an exception

.....................

**else:**

This block is executed if there is no exception.


**Some facts related to syntax:**

- There may be a number of except statements for a single try statement.
- It is particularly useful when there are statements in the try block throwing different kinds of exceptions.
- The else block code is executed when an exception is not raised by the try:block code.
- The code that does not require the try:block's protection can be included in the else-block.

**The example** below represents a simple example in which a file is opened and the content is written and also comes out without any problem:

**#!/user/bin/www/python**

**try:**

**fh = open("targetDocument", "w")**

**fh.write("I am using target document  for handling the exception")except IOError:**

**print "Message: there is no file or read data"**

**else:**

**print "Successfully added the content to the document"**

**fh.close()**

Following result will be produced:

**Successful in writing the content  to the file**

**Example:**

The example given below performs the function of opening a file where there is no permission of writing in the file, so an exception is raised:

**#!/user/bin/www/python**

**try:**

**fh = open("targetDocument", "w")**

**fh.write("I am using target document  for handling the exception")**

**except IOError:**

**print "Message: there is no file or read data"**

**else:**

**print "Successfull in writing the content to the file"**

The below result would be produced:

**Message: there is no file or read data**

The except statement without exceptions might also be used as is described below in the event of exceptions by the except clause

**try:**

**You will perform all your operations here;**

**………………….**

**except:**

**If any exception is found, then the block code will be executed.**

**If there is a case of exception, then the execution of the block code takes place**

**………………….**

**else:**

**Execute the block as no exception is found.**

All the exceptions that occur are caught by this type of try-except statement.

**Multiple exceptions except clause:**

The same except statement might be employed for handling more than one exceptions as described below:

**try:**

**Your operations are done here;**

**.....................**

**except(Exception1[, Exception2[,...ExceptionN]]):**

**If the given exception list has an exception, this block is executed**

**.....................**

**else:**

**Execution of this block takes place in the case where there is not any exception.**

**The try-finally clause:**

A finally:block might be used with a try:block. The following represents the try-finally statement's syntax.

Your operations are done here;

.....................

This can be skiped because of any exception

finally:

Execution of this will always take place

......................It should be noted that the except clause(s) can be provided, but both can not be provided. The else and finally clause can not be used.

**Example:**

**#!/usr/bin/www/python**

**try:**

**fh = open("targetDocument", "w")**

**fh.write("I am using target document  for handling the exception")**

**finally:**

**print "Message: there is no file or read data"**

If we cannot access the document in the writing mode,the following output will be given:

**Error: there is no file or read data**

You can write the same example in a cleaner manner:

**#!/usr/bin/www/python**

**try:**

**fh = open("targetDocument", "w")**

**try:**

**fh.write("I am using target document for handling the exception")**

**finally:**

**print "File will be closed soon"**

**fh.close()**

**except IOError:**

**print "Message: there is no file or read data"**

When you throw an exception on the try block, the execution is immediately passed to the finally block. After the execution of all the statements that are in the finally block, the exception raises again and the except statements handle it if they are present the try except statement's higher layer.

**An Exception's argument:**

An exception may also have an argument. An argument can be considered as a value that delivers extra information for a problem. An argument's content is altered by exception. The argument of an exception can be captured when a variable in the except clause is supplied as shown in the example below:

**try:**

**Your operations are done here;**

**.....................**

**except ExceptionType, Argument:**

**An arguement's value can be printed here...**

If a code for handling a single exception is written, there can be a variable following the exception's name in the except statement. If multiple exceptions are trapped, there might be a variable following the exception's tuple. If trapping of multiple exceptions takes place, there might be variable following the exception's tuple.

The exception's value can be received by the variable that mostly contains the exception's cause. Multiple or single values can be received by the variable in the form of a tuple. Usually, the error (string, number, location) can be contained by the tuple.

Below represents a single exception's example:

**#!/usr/bin/www/python**

**# Defining a function.**

**def change(variable):**

**try:**

**return int(variable)**

**except ValueError, Argument:**

**print "No numbers are found in the argument", Argument**

**change("abch");**

Following result will be produced when the above function is called on the above line:

**Zero numbers are present in the argument**

**literal not valid for int() with base 10: 'abcd'**

## How to raise exceptions:

Exceptions can be raised by several methods with the help of the raise statement. There are a number of ways in which an exception can be raised. The following is a representation of the raise statement syntax:

**raise [Exception [, args [, traceback]]]**

In this case, the argument corresponds to the exception argument's value. In case where an argument is not given, it is declared as none as it is completely optional to supply argument.

## Example:

An exception might be an object, a string or a class. It is very simple to define new exceptions and it might be done as follows:

**def NameOfFunction( stage ):**

**if stage < 1:**

**raise "Not a valid stage", stage**

**#the code following to this will not be executed**

It is to be noted that for catching an exception, the "except" clause should be referred to the same exception that is thrown be it object, class or simple string. To exemplify, for capturing the exception given above, the except clause can be given as:

**Game Logic...**

**except "Improper stage!":**

**Here we will handle the exception...**

**else:**

**Following code will be executed...**

### User-Defined Exceptions:

There is also the flexibility of the creation of exceptions by the user in python. This is done by derivation of classes from the built in exceptions that are the standardized.

Below is an example in relation to the runtime error. This example makes a class that has been subclassed from the runtime error. It is helpful when more specific information is required to be display in the event of an exception being caught.